Heaven Can Wait

Words

That Inspire, Motivate and Entertain

by

Joseph G. Kalil, DDS

Heaven Can Wait

Words

That Inspire, Motivate and Entertain

by

Joseph G. Kalil, DDS

PEAR
TREE
PUBLISHING

Heaven Can Wait

Words that Inspire, Motivate and Entertain

By Joseph G. Kalil, DDS
Copyright © 2016 by Joseph G. Kalil

Published by Pear Tree Publishing
An imprint of Obert Publishing
Bradford, Massachusetts
www.PearTreePublishing.net

First Edition
Proudly printed in the United States of America

Kalil, Joseph
Heaven Can Wait / by Joseph G. Kalil, DDS – 1ˢᵗ Ed.

ISBN 978-1-62502-009-3
Library of Congress Control Number: 2016935757

1. Poetry – Author. 2. Poetry – New England. 3. Poetry – American
I. Title II. Kalil, Joseph

The Dentist's Prayer by Joseph G. Kalil, DDS
"The Dentist's Prayer," © 1991 American Dental Association, Reprinted with permission.

Cover & Book Design by Joseph G. Kalil and Christopher P. Obert
Cover photos by Joseph G. Kalil & Christopher P. Obert
Author photo by Mikaela Carrozza
2,3,4,5,6,7,8,9,10

Dedication

To My Dear Family and Friends

May the thoughts expressed in this book never be forgotten.

Table of Contents:

10

Introduction

Not your typical book of poetry!

The object of this book is to entertain as well as to inform, motivate and inspire readers with stories taken from personal experiences, travel, as well as a philosophy of life and living that is truly engaging. It is an unorthodox collection of poems and stories that I have written over the years that people have enjoyed and prompted me to write a book on. The book speaks to a philosophy and lifestyle that says life is worth living. Most of the topics are presented in a poetic form that is easily understood. I hope you will find this work uplifting, informative and thought provoking.

Learn, Laugh, Cry, Enjoy, and above all Smile and Be Happy.

Joseph G. Kalil

"Smiling has the power of relaxing the mind,
delighting the heart, boosting the immune system,
slowing the heartbeat and breathing rate."
Dr. T. P. Chia View

Acknowledgments

My sincere thanks to Karen Hayden, Executive Director of Methuen Cable Television (MCTV), Methuen, MA, for her timely suggestions and scholarly review of my entire manuscript. A member of the Grey Court Poets, she authored "Bringing Up the Rear", a series of articles for Revolutionary War re-enactors and edited her professional association's newsletter.

I would be remiss if I did not mention how the influence of my participation in the activities of the Grey Court Poets in Methuen, MA prompted me to move forward with this endeavor. The positive reviews of Gayle C. Heney and Kelley Last were very encouraging.

Sincere thanks to artist & graphic designer Carol Boileau for her talented input on the cover and book design.

Also, to Christopher Obert of Pear Tree Publishing for his input and dedication to the success of this poetry book. I am indebted to Chris for his knowledge on book publishing and his patience and attention to details.

To my wife Helen, thank you for your patience and support during this entire effort. Your comments and ideas were very much appreciated. Thank you to all my family and friends who urged me on to write this book.

"Do one thing every day that makes you happy."
Unknown

Heaven Can Wait

So much to do

Before passing through

That Golden Gate

Heaven Can Wait

Aging

"I am not afraid of aging,
but more afraid of people's reactions to my aging."
Barbara Hershey

Aging

The process of aging commences at birth,
Never ceases until we enter the earth.
When awake, and as we slumber,
Each day passes, another number.

From childhood days to adolescent,
We travel each stage, we reach its crescent.
Hastening through the age of consent,
Rapidly reaching the years of content.

Always seeking to make an impression,
Showing ones age with much discretion.
Dressing carefully to keep in style,
Striving to always fashion a smile.

In spite of all the vigilant care,
Changes take place that are hard to bear.
The man in the mirror is not quite the same,
And surely there is no one else to blame.

I contemplate when the hour will come,
Always grateful when each day is done.
My dream when I have traveled each stage,
Is to die young – at a very old age!

A Senior's Lament

How is it that I am living
As I see other people die
My life goes on in spite of illness
How can it be?

If we are all created equal
This specimen called man
Why not leave this earth together
How can it be?

This machinery of our body
So complicated as it is
Does not last forever
How can it be?

Modern medicine does wonders
To restore life for so many
Yet for others the time has come
How can it be?

We are here for Him
Who created this earth and sun
As caretakers we labor until our day is done.

Difficult to understand when the time arrives
Why others pass on and we continue to survive
How can it be?

Decades of My Life

At ten years old I traveled on my roller skates
Up and down the streets.
I looked inside the grocery windows,
And watched the butcher cut meats.

At twenty I drove my uncle's car,
And had learned to ride a bike.
Then it was in the Army,
Where I took my first long hike.

At thirty, finished riding subways and trains,
Raising children to be adults.
It really challenged our brains,
Keeping them on track and away from cults.

In my forties I owned two cars,
One for work and one for play.
When the weather was fine I would ride my bike,
For work was just a mile away.

Athletic at fifty with sports of any kind,
Working out at any time of the day.
It was therapy for body and mind,
A lifestyle I could not betray.

At sixty I did all the things in decades past,
Probably the best time of my life had arrived.
With the exception that it wasn't quite as fast,
I often wonder how I survived.

Soon seven decades will transpire,
Strength and balance have not perished.
Still filled with inspiration and desire,
Memories will remain and be cherished.

Decades of My Life – A Sequel

The seventh decade has arrived
I can't believe I am still alive
Uncertain surprises lie ahead
Some of which I really dread

Seventy years went fleeting by
Like a shooting star in the sky
A streak of events too many to list
Some of which will never be missed

At eighty now I have reached Old Age
I see things change that just seem strange
Who knows what these years will bring
I cannot think of a single thing

Nine decades is not an unreasonable goal
For sure by now I will really look old
There will be many changes I will never see
It probably was never meant to be

Eighth Decade of My Life

At eighty now, I have reached old age.
Who knows what this year will bring?
They say it does not get any better,
    It is no longer spring.

For many it is the final season.
I struggle with the usual chores.
As ailments strike more often,
    There seems to be less cures.

We go through phases in our life,
Our body tells us what we can do.
There will still be many challenges,
    It is entirely up to you.

Nine decades is not an unreasonable goal.
There will be many more things to see,
Surely there will be someone there
    To record the events for me.

Beatitudes for the Aged

Blessed are they
Who stop and take the time to chat for awhile.
Blessed are they
Who make it known that I am still loved and respected.
Blessed are they
Who looked away when I spilled my cup of coffee.
Blessed are they
Who repeat what they say for my strained ears to hear.
Blessed are they
Who listen to the wisdom of my life experiences.
Blessed are they
Who laugh with me although my jokes are not funny.
Blessed are they
I do not recognize, for my eyes are dim like morning fog.
Blessed are they
Who understand my faltering step and shaking hand.
Blessed are they
Who know that my wits are slow and patiently just listen.
Blessed are they
Who walk with me although the pace is terribly slow.
Blessed are they
Who shake my hand and kiss me on the cheek.
Blessed are they
Who help me find my eyeglasses, wallet and my keys.

For they all shall dwell forever
In my heavenly kingdom of family and friends.

Doing Ok

My wife said my memory is failing
Not the only thing that is ailing.
Lost my glasses and keys to the car
I can't seem to remember where they are.

My doctor says I have arthritis in my joints
Probably right from many different points.
I have put on some weight, I used to be thin
But I'm doing okay for the shape that I'm in.

Living with Parkinson's for over 10 years
Yet better off than many of my peers.
Back surgeries and a hernia have slowed me down
I'm doing okay with the pain - I just frown.

I am told quite often I need a hearing test
I answer okay and you know the rest.
Cataracts in both eyes and my vision is dim
But I'm doing okay, I still go to the gym.

Every morning I wake up with pain in my back
Something there must be out of whack.
Many sleepless nights thinking of tomorrow
Is there any more time that I can borrow?

"How are you doing?" people ask each day.
With a smile I simply answer —

"I'm doing OK."

Growing Up

A product of our parents as we all know
Not possible to foresee how we will grow
Short or tall, large or small,
No one really knows at all.

We look in the mirror and what do we see?
Body changes occurring we cannot control
Each different than yesterday
Just a part of growing old.

My ears like TV Dishes
Flop on each side
For as you can see
They have no place to hide.

I'm sorry one eye
Won't open when I try
My doctor says
Because it is dry.

The hair hangs down
From the back of my neck
While on the top of my head
There isn't a speck.

The bump on my head
Is not half as bad
As the bump on my belly
For that I am glad!

Can't see my feet
Just below my nose
As hard as I try
Can not touch my toes.

Thank God for my parents
For things can be worse,
That bump could be a cancer,
That would be a curse.

It Could Be Better

I get up in the morning
On two weak legs.
It could be better.

I have my juice and cereal
My back still aches.
It could be better.

I go for my walk
Around the deserted streets,
As I love to do each morning.

Afternoons I take my nap
I feel very tired.
It could be better.

We go out for dinner
Relaxing with a glass of wine,
Hoping that tomorrow
It will be better.

But then again,
It could be worse.

My Eyeglasses

As I ponder where my new eyeglasses went
And the amount of time that I have spent
Searching in every place I can recall
Yet having no real luck at all.

Is it age or an illness I have acquired
Or some event unknown transpired?
In any event I am keeping my sanity
Holding my breath with no profanity.

I have resorted to prayer and went to church
To petition Saint Anthony in my desperate search
It was shocking to learn our pastor had lost his too
And our prayers to date had not come through.

I have looked everywhere near and far
In every room and car and bar
So I continue to search and in my quest
I have hope to find them and come to rest.

Then I will need to make one more stop
And take them back to the optical shop
Not simply to ascertain their description
But to correct an error in my prescription.

Petition

Get well soon my love
We have a road to travel
We have not reached our finish line
The road is thick with gravel.

A very short distance to our goal
We are not very far
Markers are no longer on the road
Remember where we are.

Spectators gather all around
They just came for a visit
I hold her hand as we move on
And I wonder what is it?

Difficulty breathing
No strength remains in the feet
She struggles with each step
Energy dissipated into the street.

We looked for help
But none could be found
There is no answer
We have looked around.

I hold her hand
We are almost home
Again she shakes it loose
And strives to do it on her own.

There is a bench
Let us sit and rest
Then perhaps we can carry on
For we have done our very best.

Just a few more things to do and see
O Lord, just let it be.

The Demon Within

Where did he come from?
That beast that haunts me each day
He roams around my body
Inviting me to play.

I tried to quickly move my hand
But something held me back
Like a limiting elastic band
That my strength could not attack.

Fingers across the keyboard
No longer smooth or fast
Could that ever be restored
Or is this concert the last?

The sound of music ceased
One finger continued to play
At rest upon my knee
It slowly tapped away.

It would be wonderful to read
That newspaper as I planned
If only I can be freed
Of that tremor in my hand.

So I walk a little slower now
With a little dancers shuffle
Yes, faster do I vow,
Till it makes my feathers ruffle.

I speak, the voice is weak
In my thoughts, there is delay
Even at my very peak they ask,
What did you say?

We know not his name
This demon that roams my soul
Nor from where he came
Or actions he can control.

He devours my strength
And confuses my mind,
He goes to great length
Destroying answers that I find.

There is rigidity in my facial expression
I just take everything in stride
Struggling to change with great discretion
But I have nowhere to hide.

"As many as one million Americans live with Parkinson's disease, which is more than the combined number of people diagnosed with multiple sclerosis, muscular dystrophy and Lou Gehrig's disease." – Parkinson's Disease Foundation

What Did You Say?

The games were exciting, we cheered every goal,
Did this yelling and screaming finally take its toll?

I love to sing, and recall my days in the choir,
When our voices echoed through the church spire.

The choral group concerts with full orchestration,
Were the highlights of my music and its culmination.

In the classroom, students understood each word,
It was apparent the message was clearly heard.

Leadership was a successful part of my career,
In every dissertation they listened and did hear.

Then the dreaded question, "What did you say?"
Began to haunt me more frequently each day.

"Speak up I can't hear you" was a common request,
In spite of my efforts to do my very best.

Now, I practice my loud voice each day,
So people will stop asking, "What did you say?"

Old Age

Old age I decided is a gift
It takes a lifetime to achieve
I never really thought of it as a goal
Until I started to feel like I was getting old.

So much hair collecting on my brush
I really never noticed it before
Perhaps it's the new lens in my eye
That I can't see as well anymore.

What did you say my dear?
Please turn up the TV
It does not sound very clear
There must be more wax in my ear.

Hurry, there is someone at the door
Sorry, I can't go fast anymore
With age there is not very much to gain
Being too aggressive only brings pain.

Who cares, I have reached my goal
I see joy in growing old
I am free to do as I please
Though it is not with the greatest of ease.

Blessed to have lived long enough
So tired of putting up with old stuff
For the first time I truly do see
The person I never wanted to be.

Entertaining

"You don't stop laughing when you grow old,
you grow old when you stop laughing."
George Bernard Shaw

A Dream

Hard to believe what I can see
From my vantage point up here in the sky
So much higher than the tallest tree
What if something should go awry?

Gliding over mountains of clouds so free
Wind howls and rushes across my face
There is no other place I would rather be
A feeling of freedom as I hurdle through space.

A sense of exhilaration as I glide through the air
Soaring like a bird as if my arms had wings
Rising, gliding downward, flying on a prayer
Real or imagined it is the strangest of things.

Eyes open wide yet the dream still clings
Memory is fading and the end draws nigh
It is the strangest of things
Vision so clear- I thought I could fly!

All That Glitters

A snowflake floating down from the sky,
A tear drop in a little boy's eye,
An icicle framed by a windowpane,
An autumn leaf glimmering in the rain.
You see, all that glitters is not gold,
So I'm told.

Birth of a Poem

Letters dancing around in the globe
A lottery of words hoping to be found
I stare, my eyes probe and I wonder
Will it shatter and fall to the ground?

I reach in and quickly grab one
Do you think it would be absurd?
All I really want to do
Is just simply make a word.

A stream of air keeps them flying
They never seem to stop,
But I will never cease trying
Unless the lottery is a flop.

Pull the plug and call it quits
Let them fall to the ground
I will choose and make a word
From all that remain around.

I gather and lay them side-by-side
A very slow process indeed
To see which of them coincide
Then I finally concede.

It certainly is a play on words
An exciting sight to see
For these are the rewards
When a poem will come to be.

Bocce

Bocce is a game of sorts
Different from all the other sports
It does not require great strength or stamina
Played within a very narrow parameter.

Hand eye coordination not really required
Just bowling skills are all that is desired
No age requirements for young or old
Male or female can be enrolled.

Physically challenged can also have their day
For anyone who can roll a ball can play
It suffers from an image as an "old fogies" game
Arguing, kibitzing and finding someone to blame.

The history of Bocce is obscure
But the Joy of Bocce will endure
You can play Bocce on grass or dirt
On a sandy beach or artificial earth.

It is safe and easy to play the game
Recreational rules may not all be the same
So do not fuss when you hear them say
"That is not the way we play."

There is no dress code for this sport
Just a measuring tape to see if the toss fell short
In the fields and yards, the clubs and halls
All you need to play Bocce – is Balls.

Champions

They stood tall with arms raised
Motionless as their eyes gazed
Staring up at the sky
When the music played.

The roar of the crowd
Created a medley of sound
While they glided like ballerinas
Spinning and twisting around.

Blades of steel creating patterns of snow
Cutting through the frozen waters below
Soon fade away and vanish in time
Unable to be etched in the frozen brine.

Look here my friends and pay close attention
Look how artistic, the technical I won't mention
The music ceased, they stood motionless again
The roar of the crowd acclaimed them champions.

Excuses

I am sorry my nose
Is in the front of my head.
But what other place
Could it be instead?

Wake up each day,
Hard to get dressed,
So after some time,
I just sit down and rest.

I should go to the gym
And work out each morning,
By the time I decide,
I am back in bed snoring.

That is the way I am.
I find it hard to decide,
It is not for the lack of effort
For I have really tried.

All my plans for the day
Have gone down the drain.
I just keep making excuses,
I am losing my brain.

One for the Road

There is nothing wrong
With a glass of wine,
Or perhaps two
Would be even better.
I feel good now,
I'm really not under the weather.

Perhaps something to eat
Would be fine
Before one more glass of wine.
I'm sure everything
Will be okay,
Although there may be a price to pay.

The music is so loud
I can hardly hear.
I really feel wonderful, but
My head is about to explode.
There is not much left in the bottle,
Perhaps I can have one more for the road!

Senses

There are many senses that we all enjoy
God given senses we all employ
Touch, taste, vision, smell and sound
Gifts that help us experience the world around.

Who knows how many more senses we use
And what about the ones that we abuse?
Psychologists are only beginning to explore
Imagination as one of many others, I am sure.

As in the birth of a child a sight to see
The cry announcing it is to be
The joy of holding him in your hands
Comes through these senses as I understand.

From all of these, we make decisions
We plan ahead with all our visions
We touch, we taste, we look and listen
Yet find it hard to make a decision.

A sixth sense finally comes around
An intuitive one not yet found
From which all of these we can condense
To the most important one called common sense!

Family

"The bond that links your true family is not one of blood,
but of respect and joy in each other's life."
Richard Bach

Meet My Children

Catherine

The first and oldest child
Leader of the clan
Keeps after her mother
When she gets out of hand.

Kenneth

He was also born in Philadelphia
Now the leader of the bunch
Where his life is heading
I don't have a hunch.

Christina

We never use that name – it's Tina
Three syllables is just too much
I believe Tina is mom's favorite girl
But very sensitive to the touch.

Carol

A wife, a mother, and teacher
Who has an outline for everything she does
But even with all this planning
She is always in a buzz.

Kevin

Our baby who is constantly deep in thought
Always has an answer — smartest one around
But we can never find him
Since birth, he is always out of town.

A Great Grandfather

A new title was bestowed on me today
For an achievement I had no part to play.
It is an honor few people in life receive
Since it takes so much time to achieve.

It comes with a basic premise of love
Blessed by the Holy Spirit above.
Years go by for it to nourish
But only moments for it to flourish.

There are requirements to reach this goal
One of them is growing old.
There must be children to carry the banner
Surely it's someone who is a planner.

Father and Grandfather are titles that inflate,
But there is nothing better than a Grandfather
That is Great!

Helen

Those wonderful moments that we shared
Dancing across the ballroom floor
They will never be forgotten
For I always wanted more.

More time to spend together
Only wonderful thoughts remained
As I left to serve my country
Our love for each other was strained.

The joy of holding you in my arms
And the thrill of our first kiss
Moments together in all the places
Is what I really missed.

Our dreams were shared in the starlit sky
While we were far apart
Wishing all our dreams come true
Our hope from the very start.

The wonderful journey now nears its end
What a fantastic life we have been through.
Together now we can truthfully say
"All of our dreams have come true!"

Kelley

Her skin was soft and tanned, her eyes were a deep dark brown, she had a beautiful smile – her face was without a frown. Her lips were a natural red and her hair was long and dark, I listened to her laugh – she always had a spark.

The sad news came one day and it was very unexpected. The doctors said it was true – she had to follow what they had directed. The days went by so slowly for they needed confirmation, she hoped everything would be OK – for she neared her graduation.

The treatment plan was made and the family sat and listened, it would be a very long year – for with many drugs she would be christened. It was not very long before her skin turned from tan to white, her brown eyes sort of yellowed, but her smile was still so bright.

Her lips are pink and dry, and her hair is now all gone, yet though her voice is weak – her words are like a song. All her friends and family wait with anxious anticipation, and marvel at her amazing grace, which has given them inspiration.

Yes, it will be a very long year, and as we pass through each season, we continue to hope and pray - but may never know the reason. The day will soon arrive with hope and faith and prayer, when all things will return – her smile – her tan – her hair.

Mary

Mary, this is your brother
I know you can hear me
Let us pray together
"Hail Mary full of Grace"
Her lips simply motioned the words.

The sound of Christmas music played softly
Friends and family came to visit
Interrupted only by her caretakers.
A devilish thing was taking her life away
For which there was no cure.

In spite of all the prayers and petitions
God would have his way
When I returned her eyes were closed,
As she laid motionless in her railed bed.

I reached for her hand
This time she did not bring it to her cheek
The hand of God was in its grasp.
The bells sounded
Lifting her spirit to His Heavenly Kingdom.

Farewell

When Does Life Begin?

It seems that it was not too long ago
That I watched my little children grow
The girls and boys, they crawled then walked
They giggled and laughed and soon they talked.

There was a great demand for our attention
The toys, the food, I need not mention
They slowly grew old enough for school
And those were the times we had to pool.

It was meetings and sports
And reviewing reports
Proms and parties all along the way
Then the final step, the final day.

They made their choice for college
Hopefully to gain more knowledge
An investment well worthwhile
Tuition that does not make parents smile.

Marriage and Careers have taken them away
Perhaps they will return again some day
No longer do we hear their cries
Or have to contend with their innocent lies.

So when does life begin for us?
It is a subject we need to discuss
It is when the children leave home, I surmise
And the family dog finally dies.

Holidays

"Holidays are about experiences and people,
and tuning into what you feel like doing at that moment.
Enjoy not having to look at a watch."
Evelyn Glennie

Christmas

Flowers wilt as woodlands cease to grow
Holidays and Holydays consume our time
Autumn leaves soon covered by the snow
Leave footsteps where people shop and dine.

Which of these is Christmas meant to be?
A festival, a legal day off is what it has become
Stringing lights or decorating a tree
Perhaps just vacation time for some.

Santa with his red suit and white beard
Reindeer with a sleigh full of toys
Shoppers seeking treasures
These distractions often destroy.

The true meaning of "Christ" in Christmas,
That is what it was meant to be.
The reindeer, toys and Santa Claus
Are wonderful to see.

Yes, He is the Savior of the world
Who has come to set us free.
Remember our greatest gift this day
Is not what is under the tree.

From a Father on Father's Day

Good morning all my children
On this beautiful Father's Day.
I know you have been thinking,
How can we repay?

Repay me for all the things I've done
And I hope I've done them well.
Well let me reassure you,
There's no way that I can tell.

A gift certificate to my favorite store
Or some new electronic device.
A pair of pants or shirt and tie,
A new cologne – that would be nice.

All of these things are wonderful,
I really don't need them anymore.
My old clothes don't seem to wear out,
But I still enjoy them for sure.

What I love most on Father's Day
Is to hear of your success,
Of your accomplishments,
Your agenda for the future, and all the rest.

So come and visit today
And tell me what you plan to do.
When you leave and say goodbye,
Just remember to say "I Love You."

Holidays

Holidays are here again
    A time when friends and families meet

Over the sacrificial lamb – the Turkey
    They feast and give Thanks-giving

Little children wander through the streets
    Classrooms will soon close

Indicative of the season when
    Halloween costumes are stowed

Days are much shorter now
    Time changes bring early sun and long dark days

All have thoughts of Christmas time
    As festive lights glitter in the falling snow

You know that the Christ Child will soon arrive
    A premonition of this Holy Day
    When He soon becomes the

Sacrificial Lamb

Inspirational

"Believe in yourself! Have faith in your abilities!
Without a humble but reasonable confidence in your own
powers you cannot be successful or happy."
Norman Vincent Peale

ASAP

There's work to do,
Deadlines to meet,
You've got no time to spare.
But as you hurry and scurry,
Always say a prayer.

In the midst of family chaos,
Quality time is rare. ·
Do your best,
Let God do the rest,
Always say a prayer.

It may seem like your worries,
Are more than you can bear.
Slow down and take a breather,
Always say a prayer.

God knows how stressful life is,
He wants to ease our cares.
And he will respond "As Soon As Possible"
Always Say A Prayer.

Being a Nurse

A great opportunity to serve mankind
Now blessed with the healing hands
It took time, courage and hours of study
But you have completed your plans.

Your skill and knowledge will be put to work
The challenges, they are there for you
To ease the pain and suffering
With the hope to heal them too.

You are the guardian angels
Closer than any spouse or kin
You are the inspiration for each
The battle, you want them to win.

You dispense a menu to heal the body
Your kind words help to heal the mind
And as you watch each day go by
Your hope is that they will be fine.

Then the glorious day arrives
They walk through the sliding doors
With a smile they say their goodbyes
You hope they return no more.

"What you have done for others
is how you will be remembered."

Faith vs. Knowledge

When I do not have an explanation
For a topic not clearly understood
With knowledge on the subject
If I could make it clear, I would.

When I cannot find a reason
And no one else can explain
It takes a great deal of courage
For faith to remain.

The psychological result of learning is knowledge.

Laughter

It has been called the music of life
That conducts itself for healing
Counteracting nervous tension and strife
Lending pleasures of good feeling.

Convulsing viscera stirs the spirit
To a glorious feeling of joy
As the physician of the soul
Sad feelings it does destroy.

Belly laughter brings relief
In a very special way
So make it your belief
Let it happen every day.

Frowns require more muscles
So save on energy with smiles
Less chance of engaging in tussles
Avoid all those stressful styles.

Yes, a smile is contagious
And kind words are immeasurable
Merriment need not be outrageous
For laughter to be pleasurable.

Olympic World

Children of every race and creed
Grow with knowledge and soon succeed

With great fervor, they hone their skill
Their goal is to win and not to kill

They challenge and compete in every way
Their rules are simply just fair play

Although they speak a different tongue
They sense the answer both old and young

Eyes and lips show expressions of joy
Yet pain is endured by every girl and boy

Fallen and broken as some may be
Strangers step forward to set them free

Gold, silver or bronze is everyone's goal
Winners determined by strength and soul

Three flags stand out as the very best
But none of the others are laid to rest

We know challenges will never cease
Yet on this stage, there is always peace

Imagine all this exploited and curled
Into a globe of an Olympic World.

Who Are You?

Sit down awhile and meditate
Close the doors and draw the blind
Switch off the lights and stereo
Leave all your cares behind.

Turn off the video and TV
And seek what is true reality
Not on the screen but in your mind
Do you know what you want to be?

What is it that brings you here?
Is it just who you are today,
What does the future hold for you?
Not changing, you will just decay.

Change your future with a believing goal
And make a dream come true.
It only takes a few moments of thought
The final decision is always up to you.

Heavenly

Flashes of light
Fragmenting the darkened sky
Daylight luminosity displaying
Exquisite scenes passing by.

Airstreams just brisk enough
To propel your wings and fly
With apparitions of things
That has never met the eye.

Ethereal melodies fill the air
With a harmony of song
A pungent sweet aroma
Senses that must be wrong.

Now gracefully floating over
An avenue of puffy white clouds
Wide awake yet in a coma
People appear covered with shrouds.

There stood visions of a man
That I could not erase
Surrounded by a garden
Empowering me to embrace.

As I followed in his footsteps
A voice cried out this decree
From out of the wilderness
Saying, "Come follow me."

It was a journey
That set my soul free
A glimpse of paradise
If only everyone could see.

Life

"Life is divided into three terms – that which was, which is, and which will be. Let us learn from the past to profit by the present, and from the present, to live better in the future."
William Wordsworth

Life

Of all the things I do possess,
One stands out among the rest.
Not able to be traded or sold,
Its value is greater than gold.

What is in truth most appealing?
Is the fact that it has feeling.
I cherish it each day – for I never know,
When it will be taken away.

A Life Worthwhile

If I can inspire by things that I have done
And by what I have failed to do
It makes life worth living

I am better than many people
But many people are better than I
We all have something to contribute

Your thoughts have value
No matter how big or small
They need to be expressed

Our words and our deeds
Speak for themselves
Actions being louder than words

So do not pretend
Get it done in the end
It will make for a better world

If we all had done our part
What a wonderful place this would be
So make your life worthwhile
And become a part of history

Bus Stop

Planet Earth is just a bus stop,
Where people come and go.
It can be very lonely,
Until some people show.

Where do they all come from?
Young and old, black and white
Who speak different languages,
What is their woeful plight?

I too arrived very long ago,
It has been a very pleasant stay,
Shared many friendships and adventures,
So many, many have gone away.

Transported to another world,
It seems their time had come.
I watched them leave with sadness,
Not knowing where they came from.

For years I strolled along the roadway
Of this beautiful stop called Earth,
With vehicles racing past me,
Seeking to find my berth.

Cup of Life

Life is an empty glass to be filled,
With little time to do it.
If you can reach the brim, be thrilled,
Quickly grab another cup and fill it.

Hold steadfast to that fragile crystal,
For it can fall and shatter.
No matter how full that cup or glass,
If it breaks, it doesn't matter.

Then all of life's milestones
Will be lost in your history.
You will never be remembered,
Your days will remain a mystery.

Emma

My son, you gave me such a gift,
A baby girl, my first grandchild.
So close to my heart, then soon to drift,
Pushed by a force unseen and wild.

I look at her and I see me,
Hazel eyes that mirror my face.
Please come, do not flee,
Must there always be such space?

I love you grammie, says she,
As we play pirate ship on the rock.
Will I ever find the key
For the answers to unlock?

You are my sunshine Emma,
Let us hold hands and walk.
We suffer a real dilemma,
We cannot even talk.

Twisting and turning her braided hair,
At the frog pond her eyes would gleam,
Dressing her doll with garments and flair,
Are all now just a dream.

He has closed the door forever,
I will never know the reason why.
As I drive past the house,
All I can do is cry.

Have a Heart

A mass of muscle
About the size of a fist
Pulsating at the center of living organs,
Designed for the task of sustaining life.

Not so intricate
That it cannot be duplicated.
Heart valves miraculously fabricated,
Preserve blood flow and the beats go on.

There is more to this heart
Than just this tangible mass,
Voids filled with senses not seen by the eye
Chambers of sadness, joy, rage and despair.

The generator of power,
Our source of survival
Between life and death,
A repository for love.

A fountain of life that we must treasure,
Take care of your heart
It is the source of life's pleasure.

Healing

Oh, how I wish I could feel better.
Wake up each morning feeling under the weather,
I take my medication and hope and pray
That healing will come soon one day.

My mind is clear and the pain has eased
For a while, I am really pleased.
I have been healed, of that I'm sure
Even though there is no cure.

And if a cure should happen one day,
For that I always hope and pray,
I know that I will die for real,
I always remember that God does heal.

Health & Poetry

Your doctor says you're ok
You believe your health is fine
Yet there are sleepless nights
That leaves you in a bind

You must look in other directions
To find answers as to how you feel
For laboratory tests alone
Are indicators that are not real

We search for a state of well-being
Not just the absence of pain
The void filled with poetry and music
Can help relieve the strain

Just remember how health is described
And let it be your guide
"A state of Mental, Physical, Social
And Spiritual Well-being"
Is how it is defined

Understanding Health

Now what does that have to do with Poetry?

The World Health Organization (WHO) states:
"Health is a state of complete physical, mental and social well-being and not merely the absence of disease or infirmity." Psychologists have added the word spiritual to the definition.

So it seems, you are not healthy if simply all your laboratory reports are normal, but you cannot handle stress, have difficulty sleeping and associating with people and no appreciation of nature.

Poetry and music help fill the gap toward well-being. Poetry is one of the most unique and compelling of art forms. It is a concert of words that is orchestrated to create positive images, or tell a story. Music is what feelings sound like. Poetry is what feelings look and feel like. Good nutrition, exercise, life style and prayer fill the void to nourish the body and the spiritual soul. Poetry is another venue towards happiness and health.

Joy of Running

In spring, summer,
Winter or fall
At any time
Of the year at all

Stresses are channeled
Into the earth
From pounding feet
Compressing the dirt

It is the sweat
That cleanses the body
Flushing the venom
No longer shoddy

As the beat goes on
To a faster pace
The hope is just
To finish the race

At the end of the day
There is great delight
Completing this journey
Was quite a plight

Kindness

Kindness is not a feeble virtue
Found only in the very weak
For compassion lies within the power
Of both the mighty and the meek.

Machinery of My Body

They said I might need a valve job.
What the hell do you expect?
It has been running 24 –7 for over 80 years.

My damned Toyota rusted away
In a matter of three years.
They were able to recycle and replace.

Perhaps I could be so fortunate,
A repair job or just find the right parts.
Anything to preserve this laboring heart.

Where do I go from here?
Fuel pump is still working,
So let's just go with the flow.

Thanks to my maker who created this machine.
He did a nice job for which I am grateful.
I will care for it for the rest of my life

For that reason I will be faithful.

My Clock

It is a very special gift my clock,
There is none like it in the world
Created by two wonderful people
Whose love suddenly unfurled.

It tells not the time of day
Neither second, minute or hour
The sun rises and sets
Daylight restores her power.

The tick goes on with a thumping sound
All through the day and night
How long it will last is the question
The answer is not in sight.

My Friend Bill

Full of laughter, intelligent and analytical.
He had his own opinion, but never political.
A tough Marine with a very big heart,
Common sense solving problems whenever he took part.

No enemies, just friends were all the people he knew,
A likeable man willing to accept your point of view.
A scientific mind that helped send the shuttle into space,
Settled arguments among people with such simple grace.

Service to others was his outstanding trait,
Wounded Warriors, sick and elderly were all on his plate.
He balanced his life between work and play,
Set an example for us to follow each and every day.

Always ready to lend a helping hand,
For the most difficult problems he would find a plan.
He loved to play golf, 45's his favorite game of cards,
But the sport of Bocce was closest to his heart.

So we dedicate this day to our friend Bill
And for all that he hoped for
We will try to fulfill.

Rocky Ledge Shores Remembered

My home away from home
Began many years ago
It was a time for camping that we did forgo.

Stay here for a week this year perhaps
It would be a nice change for you indeed
Talked it over with family and we all agreed.

Received a call a few weeks later
Another unit was for sale
Returned so as not to let this opportunity fail.

We enjoyed the spring and summer
The winters seemed so long
We will miss the colorful foliage in the fall.

Over thirty years have passed us by
Another phase in life comes to an end
Changes are often very difficult to comprehend.

We will always remember the sunsets
The early morning fog and dew
But especially, all the people that we knew.

Stillborn

As I reflect on the months gone by,
Nine months to be exact – I cry.
I recall the joys before the sorrow,
When I could hardly wait until tomorrow.

As in a garden, the seed was sown,
Nourished by a body that is full-grown.
Each day new cells are born,
Taking on a specific form.

A face, a limb, a body molded
Out of a genetic plan that has unfolded.
There must be a channel for it to flourish,
A cord that it needs to nourish.

Lub-dub, the sound of life appears
Weak and feeble, but brings joyous tears.
Suddenly each limb frantically struggles and twists,
But the tightening, strangling cord persists.

How terrible for her it must be,
To have felt the life one will never see.

The Examination

Why should it create such stress,
A simple word like exam?
It's an assessment of your knowledge,
Just do the best you can.

Simply a set of questions,
Putting you to the test.
If you have done your homework,
With success you will be blessed.

But it is never finished,
For learning never ends.
We will always be tested,
In the classroom and by our friends.

So settle down and listen,
And balance your life with cheer.
You will never have all the answers,
Nor cure the stress with beer.

Let each Exam be another challenge,
Of your knowledge and your skill.
Worry not about the grade or score,
Or have it change your will.

TIME - A Precious Gift

It may not be the greatest gift
Those moments we all possess
It is what makes the world tick
And something we must address.

Once it is gone
It can never be replaced
Each second we must capture
Lest it is fallen into waste.

Each moment takes on a new title
As it passes along the way
The moment called now
Soon becomes yesterday.

These times pass us quickly
They are gifts we cannot borrow
Since the time we call now
Is quickly replaced by tomorrow.

Reflect on yesterday and extract
What you need to set your goal
Complete your tasks in this present time
Never look back or lose control.

Villanelle of Life

Many have come and gone.
The days travel by so fast,
Life is like a marathon.

Resting only dusk till dawn,
A distance that seems so vast,
Many have come and gone.

From the race some have withdrawn,
What's wrong with coming in last?
Life is like a marathon.

And we sprint across the lawn,
In spite of those who have past,
Many have come and gone.

Lift your spirit and carry on,
Let not your sails down the mast,
Life is like a marathon.

Stand tall like the swan,
Who may not be as fast.
Many have come and gone,
Life is like a marathon.

Love

"Love has no desire but to fulfill itself.
To melt and be like a running brook that sings its melody
to the night. To wake at dawn with a winged heart
and give thanks for another day of loving."
Khalil Gibran

A Love Affair

'Twas not the first time we met that night
When the music filled the air
The stage was set, the atmosphere just right
I didn't have a care.

Lost in the crowd in the female grounds
I paced the ballroom floor
Hoping to be seen making the rounds
Only to find she was not there anymore.

Her hand reached out as if she were blind
We embraced in the traditional dance
Our cheeks touched, I tried to read her mind
I wondered if I would ever have a chance.

The grasp of her fingers
Sent tingles down my spine
In my memory, it still lingers
I knew she was mine.

Never Lonely

I have a friend
I never knew how dear
Such a short time together
Departed for more than a year

Nights were dark and sad
But one bright star in the sky
Always caught my attention
For it never passed by

We were oceans apart
Never felt very much alone
Since we shared the twinkling star
It became our stepping-stone

I will always remember those years
When we shared our emotions in the sky
With letters that we would meet again
Sometime, before I die

Our Friendship

Friends are special people
They may be difficult to choose
Making their own decision
Having very different points of views.

We have shared good times and bad
Providing us comfort and strength
It has brought us closer together
To a very great length.

Let us not forget the dreams we share
Don't let them fade away
For they are very precious
From many years ago today.

Friendship is one of life's greatest pleasure
When we did sit down and chat
Yours is one I will always treasure
My best friend Pat.

Our Relationship

Listen to what I have to say
Then you can understand.
Intercommunication is the way
Towards a life well planned.

Is it something that you fear
A social phobia of sorts?
Is it something so dear
Like a mineral of quartz?

Tell me what you feel
Our love is at stake.
Our relationship I want to seal
I do not want it to break.

Together we can share
Your life I will not control.
Do not leave me in despair
Our love just an empty bowl.

For my pleasures in life
You are the very source.
It is just a matter now
Of social intercourse.

Ryan's World

You have been there once before
An experience you will never remember
Suspended as in a liquid bowl
In darkness, like midnight in December.

It is warm and safe, I move with ease
A constant flow of energy so unreal
As water flows through a pipeline
Like nothing else that one can feel.

The time will soon arrive
When the world will change for me
As the tidewaters dwindle,
I will soon be free.

Free to meet my maker
Struggling with feelings of joy and pain
It seems like an eternity
But her efforts will not be in vain.

There are tears in her eyes
A sense of pain in the clutch of her hand
Bewilderment clouds all his emotions
He is comforting, but cannot fully understand.

As life emerges into this world
Through those methodical hands,
There must be a greater being
To have created these wonderful plans.

Happiness and joy abound
The mystery they cannot untie
Their love has now been crowned
The silence broken only by a cry.

Tragedy

I felt it in my hands
A bit of perspiration
They were warm
Then cold and clammy

I felt it in my bones
As I shuddered at the sight
My body did tremble
As it never had before

I felt it in my feet
Shoes made of lead
Held them to the floor
Unable to leave the room

I felt it in my heart
Like I had never felt it before
So fast, so loud
On a pace I could not control

I felt it in my eyes
They did not blink
Transfixed before the screen
And then a tear

I heard it in my ears
The words were very clear
Yet so hard to interpret
Maybe words I didn't want to hear

My lips quivered
There was a lump in my throat
The vision imbedded forever
In the depths of my mind.

Expressions of Love

They hugged and kissed me
And held me in their arms
I was very young and helpless
I could only sense their charms.

Unable to speak
I responded with a smile
All the pleasures and emotions
We shared all the while.

As the years went by
Expressions of love did slow
What has caused this change?
Now it is just a hello.

Today to touch or kiss
Is thought to be so strange.
It's a terrible new world,
I will never make the change!

Nature

"Live in each season as it passes;
breathe the air, drink the drink, taste the fruit,
and resign yourself to the influence of the earth."
Henry David Thoreau, Walden

Birth of a Season

As I gaze out of my window
There is amazement at what I see
The earth is multicolored
And not a leaf upon the tree.

A clump of life here and there
Makes you jump for joy
Patches of green and hints of color
Mother Nature does deploy.

As the frozen earth thaws
Creating windows for the flowers
Visions of frozen icicles
The earth now devours.

Nurtured by the warmth
Of the early morning sun
Soon over time
We know that spring has begun.

Spring

She is covered with her white winter blanket,
Buried deep down below.
So cold, perhaps she has perished?
I do not know.

Trees stand like tombstones in a graveyard,
Their limbs rigid from the wind and snow.
Is there any life left there?
I do not know.

The streams and rivers lie motionless,
In their bed of snow.
In a funeral like procession, they will begin to flow.
When? I do not know.

Tears of joy drip from rooftops,
As winter comes out of its shell.
Spring will return to the earth with splendor.
When?
Only time will tell.

One Season – Spring

What joy can there be in a single season
Where colors never change
From a monotonous scene
With a very limited range?

What pleasures can one experience
From such miniscule thermal changes
Where everything remains the same
And nature never rearranges.

Until cooled by the night and morning dew
Vegetation remains stagnant, wilting in the sun
Surviving for yet another day
Yet nothing is ever done.

The days are repetitive,
They follow the same track
Relief arrives with the sunset
Nocturnal hours remain black.

Daylight ignites the solar heat
Seeking shelter by simulated air
Intolerable moisture is vacuumed away
Cloistered in a room with no space to spare.

How can life be spirited
In this mundane way
Where nothing seems to change
From day to day?

Give me New England,
Where seasons come and go.
Four of them in fact
That brings us sun, rain and snow.

For all of these are borne from one time
A period from which all the others spring
It is the season we love the most
For all the wonders that it does bring.

Busy Bee

Every time I look to see
There is nothing but a busy bee.

All day long you never stop
Moving side to side, then to the top.

Your black and gold body is a sight to see
Traveling from branch to branch on each tree.

Hard to count your many arms and legs
Where did you come from, do you lay eggs?

What is your goal each day?
Is that all you do is play?

Siri said you transfer pollen
Without which many plants would have fallen.

As nighttime falls, do you go to sleep?
I'll bring my flashlight and take a peek.

Keep up the good work
I never did see
Such a beautiful creature as this Busy Bee.

My Favorite Animal – The Pig

The pig is an animal not often seen,
His life is very dull.
You rarely see him on the street,
Not even in a barn.
He might appear on TV or in a fairy tale,
Only to be made fun of
Because of his nose and tail.
His pudgy nose is not very pretty,
His nostrils like another set of eyes.
Head always pointed down to the ground
Constantly feeding on whatever is around.
This has caused his nose to be flattened
And his belly to be so round.
There is no other creature
Who gives all of himself like the pig,
From bacon to human heart valves,
So that life is prolonged.
I tell this tale so that we may know
Why the pig is my pride and joy
Not the prettiest of creatures
Yet in my heart – is my favorite animal.

My Garden

What is it that makes my garden grow?
Fertile land from pastures past
Planting seeds that grow so slow
Open fields so very vast.

Till the land in early spring
Nourished and fed by nature and man
Plants lined up in a perfect string
Now digest and follow the plan.

Plants and seedlings lie in wait
Parched and wilted they suffer arid pain
Elements missing that determine their fate
Anguish relieved by days of rain.

Prescriptions for growth still incomplete
Radiance lost when the day is done
Although now relieved of the latent heat
Dawn welcomes in the brilliant sun.

All the ingredients for growth are there!
Waiting for the fruit to share.

My Pear Tree

Majestic buds
Resplendent pure white flowers
A sweet ambrosia
Created by busy bees

Her limbs reach skyward
Tall like spiraled towers
Nature's picture created
With such wondrous ease

The buds conceived
From such a mating game
They shimmer in the sun
And morning dew

It is from these sprouts
The brown pears grew
That must quickly be harvested
Before ripened too soon

Like vultures, crows devour the ripened fruit
Insects and rodents consume what's on the ground
The remains fertilize and pollute
Yet, there is fruit for all of us abound

God made her for us all on earth to share,
And so is the life cycle of a pear!

My Pear Tree Died

My pear tree died this year.
I never thought I would see the day,
It was early Spring 2006.

Each morning I would glance out of my kitchen window
Hoping to catch a glimpse of the white flowering buds
That glittered in the early morning dew.

I recalled that in years past how my pear tree
Would not bear much fruit that season,
Informed that it happens only on alternate years.

I am no expert on the life cycle of a pear tree.
But neighboring trees and pollination are a necessity.
Where are those bees so necessary for this fertilization?

Perhaps I was misinformed.
In years past, I soon recalled that it was true.
Only a small bucket was harvested that Fall.

The following year several baskets were filled.
Yet many rotted on the ground or succumbed
To the appetite of crows, ants and all kinds of prey.

As summer approached I would walk out in the yard
And stroll around my tree.
There were a few embryonic buds where limbs had flowered.

By the end of summer
I came to realize there were no full-grown pears,
Not enough to fill my little pool bucket.

I felt a real sense of guilt.
I had neglected to care for my pear tree,
So I called a tree surgeon who arrived the next day.

His hand grasped at the trunk
And peeled off a piece of its bark.
"This tree is diseased" he said "and should be cut down."

My greatest fear had come to be!
It was the end for my pear tree.
Its lifeless limbs now lay on the ground.

They were the same tall branches reaching for the sky
That could no longer be trimmed
By this old guy.

The stump, like a headstone on a gravesite,
Is now all that remains.
Its surface covered with seeds of grass grains.

Come spring there will be a lawn so green,
But buried below
Will be memories serene.

Ode to Winnipesaukee

No matter what the season
You always give me reason
To be filled with pleasure
With sites that I treasure.

In spring, you are adorned with flowers
And hillsides of green.
The summer is filled with warm sunshine
And sunsets are serene.

The warm waters soothe my body,
They cleanse the sand
Adhered to my naked feet
As I stroll along the shore.

Come autumn your face fills the hillside
With shades of orange, yellow and red
Strong winds turn ripples to white caps
As leaves gather along the water's edge.

Winter comes upon you
A blanket of ice and snow,
I walk across the water
There is no place to go.

Sunset

The darkness of night is fleeting
There is nothing that the human eye can see

Suddenly I awake each morning
To the glare of the rising sun

The day filled with designer clouds
Depicts many different scenes

Yet nothing is as beautiful as the time
When the sun that sets in the evening

Turns black and white into color

Water

A painting cannot be created with pigments alone
A brush laden with water brings out art and tone
The seedling cannot germinate, or flowers come to bloom
Until they find the waters buried in earth's womb.

Riverboats held buoyant as they travel down river
Their enormous weight makes the waters shiver
Colors are created by silt and reflections of the deep,
Unlike the pigments absorbed by an artist's brush sweep.

We yearn for food and thirst for water
Soon we will die if it were not for the latter
From Mother Earth, cold waters flow
From the clouds above, they fall below.

So life endures in all earthly things
From the waters in the clouds and earthly springs
Until sister winds uncoil their power
And these same waters swell into deadly towers.

Now the liquid of life rises to enormous waves
Frothing at the mouth in a tremendous rage
All things of its kingdom erased from sight
Nothing worse ever seen from this plight.

It can give us life and take it away,
At any moment in time and no particular day.
Ice crystals divide under feverish rays of the sun
Creating colorful pools when the day is done.

Waters slowly return to their earthly domain
But somehow nothing seems to be the same.

Western Cedar

It is more than just a tree
Never seen anything like this before
It is something that one must see
A monument pleading for you to adore.

Over a thousand years old,
And more than 400 feet high,
She still stands so erect,
Branches reaching for the sky.

We make a circle around this tree
Linking hands to see what it takes
Six, seven or eight of us to encircle it
Stretching arms around her bark which never flakes.

She never pollutes – rather feeds new life,
Eagles rest in her branches and bugs in her bark
Footprints of animals leave trails to the top
They follow one another and disappear in the dark.

Many years have gone by – she doesn't want to die.
The smell of cedar is enhanced by the rain
Ferns, flowers and hemlocks now grow from her stump
She breathes new life that is hard to explain.

Snow Flakes

Walk across the field during the falling snow
Take off your hat and feel the flakes
As cold winds swirl and blow
Bear the cold for as long as it takes.

Stick out your tongue and savor the taste
Remove the muffs, uncover your ears
Do not let this time go to waste
Unwind the scarf and shed the tears.

See those autumn colors fade
Orange, red, yellow and brown
As the silver white blanket is laid
Leaves disappear from the ground.

It will not be long 'til it turns green
Enjoy these days, do not rush
Surroundings change to a different scene
As the snow slowly turns to slush.

Winter

Cold temperatures
Snow covered landscape
Warm blankets on the sofa.

White roofs and chimney smoke
Fallen trees
Icicles hanging from the roof tops.

Hot drinks on the table
Auto accidents on slippery roads
Delayed airline flights.

Snowcapped mountains
Skiers on the slopes
Children sledding down a hillside.

Ice skaters on the pond
Christmas lights everywhere
Santa Claus in his sleigh.

Children playing with new toys
Smell of the wood-burning stove
Brilliant orange flames.

Snowshoeing through the forest
Reindeer feeding in the snow
Silver cold lifeless trees.

Broken gutters and frozen pipes
Water leaks down below
Then, sounds of laughter.

Nature's Seasons

The end of a terrible winter,
That's what it really is,
Dirty streets,
Sand and salt.

Dead limbs and leaves
On trees and shrubs.
Will the earth and lawns
Ever come alive?

They shower their pollen
Into the air.
Coughing and sneezing,
Now don't despair.

Still have to keep warm,
What should I wear?
Will there be another storm?
Days go by with little change.

Now we play the waiting game,
Since before another Winter,
Comes Spring, Summer and Fall.
So let us stop
And just enjoy them all.

Prayers

"Prayer is not asking. It is a longing of the soul.
It is daily admission of one's weakness.
It is better in prayer to have a heart without words
than words without a heart."
Mahatma Gandhi

A Bedtime Prayer

Jesus, Mary and Joseph
I give you my heart and my soul.

Jesus, Mary and Joseph
Assist me in my last agony.

Jesus, Mary and Joseph
May I breathe forth my soul in peace with you
Forever in heaven.

Amen

Morning Stroll

It was very early when I left for my morning stroll.

As I approached the sandy shore, a kaleidoscope of color made an appearance across the sky, visions of a leopard moving slowly by. What creatures did he devour in the darkness of the night?

Suddenly, orange streaks like arrows launched from an archers' bow targeted the brown spots of the leopard skin then vanished out of site. The darkness faded from gray to orange to all shades of blue, the start of the transformation of day from night.

As I walked further along enjoying nature's scenes, I could see what appeared to be a garden of plantings in the field. Suddenly, there must have been a sound that I did not hear for in unison the objects did rise and the land was clear.

They spread their wings and the heavens turned white
The cackling sounds were a musical delight.
I saw feathers falling from the sky;
Or was it a brief snow shower that was passing by?

Blinded by the rising sun, I started to run.

Prayer Before Surgery

Watch over me today dear Lord
When they close my eyes
And take my breath away
My memories fade.

Bless those who watch over me
And give me life
Who heal my wounds
During these moments of strife.

Ease the worry and concern
Of family and friends
For what I need done
Is not the end.

When you gather all the prayers
Offered by all those who care
I hope it adds up
To an adequate prayer.

When light shines again
And familiar faces appear
I give thanks dear Lord
For another day down here.

Prayer After Surgery

The memory returns as I open my eyes
And breathe a sigh of relief
It was a very long time ago
Yet everything seemed so brief.

You have watched over me
And given me new life
My wounds will soon be healed
After all these moments of strife.

Ease the worry and concern
Of family and friends
For with what they have done
Life never ends.

Please continue with the offerings
All of you who care
It is never overwhelming
To contribute another meaningful prayer.

The light shines again
And everything is very clear
I give thanks dear Lord
For another day down here.

Parkinson's Prayer

Dear Pope John Paul II, for more than a quarter century you were shaping political action and moral thought. You were a victim of an attempted assassination and shortly after your recovery you responded with forgiveness to your assailant. With your suffering as a patient with Parkinson's disease you never complained. In spite of the difficulties of speech, swallowing and body movement you continued to carry the message of Christ. As weakness slowly took away your strength you continued to travel the earth. Through your examples of love and perseverance may we gain hope and strength to bear the suffering that we endure.

May the inexplicable cure of Sister Marie Simon Peirre, a French nun who was suffering from Parkinson's disease, provide the miracle required for your beatification. For those of us with Parkinson's, we pray that through your intercession we may be healed and a cure will be found. We offer our suffering in repentance for our sins and the sins of the world, so that one day we may share with you forever the blessed vision of God our heavenly Father.

We remember your wish –

"Let me go to the house of the Father."
Pope John Paul II

Saint Lucy Parish Prayer

Remember — Celebrate — Believe

O dear St. Lucy, patron saint of our parish family, your name is symbolic of your presence as the way of light. We remember your uncompromising love for Jesus. A virgin and martyr who sacrificed her physical eyes and presented them on a golden plate, miraculously was still able to see. For half a century you have been our patron and guiding light.

In this year of 2008, we **remember** and **celebrate** our growth and achievements over the past fifty years. We offer prayers of thanksgiving for your intercession. For those in our parish who suffer from problems of sight, through your intercession may they be cured.

We invoke your continued guidance. Patron Saint of the eyes, continue to be our guiding light. Inspire us with the vision to create a better tomorrow for our Saint Lucy Parish Family. Let us not be blind to all things spiritual as we prosper in our material growth. We pray and **believe** that one day we may all share with you forever the blessed vision of God our heavenly Father.

Amen

Thank You

Thank you O Lord

I saw the birds fly

I heard them sing

I smelled the roses

And tasted the wine

I sensed your touch,

Then I watched the sun set.

Thanksgiving Prayer

For our family and friends,
We give thanks today.
For those who have nothing,
We sincerely pray.

For the warmth of our home,
We give thanks today.
For the poor and the homeless,
We sincerely pray.

For the peace in our hearts,
We give thanks today.
For the war torn world,
We sincerely pray.

For the food at our table,
We give thanks today.
For those who go hungry,
We sincerely pray.

For the love that we share,
We give thanks today.
Dear lord let it grow,
Help show us the way.

For all of these gifts
That make life worth living,
Is the reason why today
Is called Thanks – giving!

What I Should Be

Oh my God,
Keep me humble and meek
That is all I ever seek.

Simply help me to be
What I should be.

I will do the rest
And in my best effort
I will strive to be the best.

Travel

"A truly happy person is
one who can enjoy the scenery while on a detour."
Author Unknown

Aruba

I traveled from the frozen tundra
To thaw my heart and soul
I never thought I would find a gem
More valuable to me than gold.

As my feet touched the silvery sands
There was a feeling never felt before
It came upon suddenly
A sensation you can not ignore.

The warm winds swept across my face
Increasing the blaze of the scorching sun
The horizon stretched far and wide
For the end there was none.

Chilled suddenly by the cooler water
Brought comfort to my soul
Strolling along the shore at sunset
The day had taken its toll.

The music played into the night
Celebrating the joy of the day gone by
I perish the thought when I must part
And have to say goodbye.

You are a magnetic pearl
You are a star in the sea
You are the beautiful mermaid
You are the place I want to be.

Fatima Pilgrimage

Near noon, the wet darkness shrouded the day
As the van traveled up the winding road,
The windshield wipers stopped their play.

Door hissed and opened – our feet touched the ground
Amidst a halo of glorious sunshine,
We slowly made our way around.

Jacinta and Francisco lived here many years ago
Tending sheep with Lucia
When the angel told them so.

It came to pass our Lady did appear,
She did talk and tell them
To pray and have no fear.

In their memory, the Shrine was built,
Millions came to pray for special favors,
To also cleanse their souls from guilt.

With candles lit and Mass attended,
The gray clouds and rain returned,
We knew the day had ended.

The memory of Fatima imprinted in my mind
Will remain forever
An experience – Divine!

On My Way

On my way home from Iceland
I met a girl named Kim,
We talked about the tulips
Dead blossoms in the spring.

We looked at photographs
Of her college in Hometown
She travels to the USA
To Vermont she is bound.

Her home is in Holland
The oldest child of five
Hoping to live in the USA
As long as she is alive.

Perhaps a job or green card
Would someday get her there
I told her what about marriage?
She laughed, being very well aware.

It made for a pleasant ride
Having a nice person by my side
Our journey will soon come to an end
Grateful to have made a very good friend.

Portugal

From Lisbon to the Algarve,
It is a gastronomic delight.
The rivers, plantations and villages,
Are a tranquil, yet exciting sight.

Sardines, octopus and squid,
Sure to be found on each menu.
Try it once they said — I did,
Indeed, a stimulating venue.

Starters of cabbage soup or salad,
Seasoned with salt from the sea,
Stimulating taste buds and palate,
With a finale of espresso or tea.

Forests of cork trees, papaya and pines,
Marzipan with almonds and figs.
Pork and fruit of all kinds,
Entrées prepared from black pigs.

Like the tuna that travels across the sea
We traveled from east to west.
Across the mountain and rivers we flee
And wait for the sunset to rest.

We carry our gifts and painted tiles
As we make our way towards Granada,
Filled with joy and faces with smiles,
Farewell dear Portugal — Obregada!

Sicily

I staggered to the open balcony,
There was not a view in sight.
No more than a black painted canvass,
Of course, it was still night.

It was just moments later,
That the sunrise pierced the sky.
The canvas now colored orange,
A spectacle only for the eye.

In the west the moon still lingered,
A mushroom cloud took form.
Was it the heat of the volcano,
Or the sign of an oncoming storm?

Below, the green gardens loomed upward,
Dwarfed by the mountains and trees.
In the distance stretched the barren horizon,
Linked together by the Mediterranean Sea.

As far and as wide as the eye can see,
No photo can capture what appears to me.
Friends gathered to dine, to talk, to play,
We will never forget this wonderful day.

Something Special

"Most of us will never do great things,
but we can do small things in a great way"
Maren Mouritsen

The Cross of Life*

Arms of the cross outstretched to each side
Standing tall from the earth to the sky
Sending a message by which we should abide
Pleading, at least, for us to try.

One word is stationed at each end
Symbolic of a way of life
Work, Play, Love and Worship
Ingredients for a world without strife.

When following all these posted paths
A lifetime of happiness ensues,
Joy and success at the end of each road
Denotes the only trails to use.

Should we fail to balance these actions
It will no longer be able to stand tall,
Excess will bring imbalance
And eventually, cause it to fall.

Each virtue is measured by the clock
Giving adequate time for each purpose
So remember the words of this cross of life,
Work, Play, Love and Worship.

Work

Love   Worship

Happiness

Play

*This image is based on Dr. Pankey's philosophy of living a balanced life. The Plankey Institute was established to promote excellence and balance in the dental profession. This philosophy is illustrated by the "Cross of Life."

A Successful Life

Have I balanced the Cross of Life
Of Work— Play— Love and Worship?
Has my work contributed to making this a better world?
Have I been an inspiration to my family and friends
And gained the respect of my fellow workers?

Have I accomplished all the tasks that I have taken up?
Have I ever taken the time to appreciate earth's beauty
And expressed it in any form as in poetry or music
So that others may be enlightened?
Did I play with my children and teach them to laugh?

Did I visit my elders and put a smile on their face?
Did I express my love with a handshake and a kiss
So they will always remember not to miss?
And finally, by example, teach them to pray
For it's worship that feeds the soul in a very special way.

Have I given the best I have
And looked for the best in others?
By example have I shown them the way?
Having done all of these things in spite of life's strife
Then I feel that I have lived
"A Very Successful Life."

Happiness

He that would find happiness
Must learn to live with the seasons

When the snow falls
Do not be discouraged

Move on my friend and start anew
Gather the straw and make your nest

Feed the little ones so hungry
See how they grow and fly

They have no fear nor worry
They soar and glide, they never hurry

Their joy is in living
Not dying

The Dentist's Prayer

Thank you O Lord,
For the privilege of being a dentist,

For letting me serve as Your instrument
In ministering to the sick and afflicted.

May I always treat with reverence
The human life which you have brought into being,
And which I serve.

Deepen my love for people
So that I will always give myself gladly and
generously
To those stricken with illness and pain.

Help me to listen patiently,
Diagnose carefully,
Prescribe conscientiously,
And treat gently.

Teach me to blend gentleness with skill,
To be a dentist with a heart as well as a mind.

Joseph G. Kalil, DDS

History of "The Dentist's Prayer"

The Dentist's Prayer, authored by Dr. Joseph G. Kalil, and read to the 127th House of Delegates meeting of the Massachusetts Dental Society (MDS) in the closing remarks of his Presidential Address. In October of 1991, after much deliberation the American Dental Association (ADA) House of Delegates, meeting in Seattle, Washington, adopted "The Dentist's Prayer" as the "Primary Parameter of Care" for Dentists. Refusing to impose rules or guidelines, it describes the manner by which all dentists should treat their patients The Resolution was submitted by the First District (Massachusetts) Dental Society.

ADA President Dr. Jack Harris presented a framed copy of "The Dentist's Prayer" to Dr. Joseph G. Kalil (right) at the annual session of the MDS House of Delegates.

The Sound of My Voice

I always enjoyed listening to talk radio. During my professional career I had the opportunity to speak to many civic organizations, as well as to appear on several radio and television programs. In 1990, I was invited to host a local radio talk show called "Let's Talk Health". The show offered the listeners a variety of informative topics on medicine and oral health. It was another exciting time in my life. I had reached a goal that had always been close to my heart. "And now the rest of the story."

The show was aired every Monday night from six to seven pm. Several months later, I was shopping at the local supermarket. I was in the produce section, when I met up with a friend. We struck up with a short conversation. As we spoke, I noticed other shoppers nearby and a middle aged woman in particular who seemed attentive to our conversation. When we parted I continued down the next aisle to check out my grocery list when I was interrupted by the same woman that caught my eye earlier. "Excuse me" she said, "Are you Dr. Kalil?" Yes, I said. "We have never met before, but I recognized your voice from your radio program. You have such a kind voice." She was a patient in our office a few weeks later convinced and comforted by the fact that she had made the right choice. Every day we influence people by those sound-bites. We educate, we console, and influence decision making for our patients. If the expression is sincere, then we most times will have succeeded.

That's the end of my story. I am convinced that it is not what we say, but how we say it that influences people. The sound of one's voice is an audible expression of ones feelings and emotions. It is the sound that comforts the child. It is the sound that disciplines the adolescent. It is the sound that comforts patients. It is the sound of my voice!

Listen. Can you hear the sound of your voice?

Biography

Dr. Joseph G. Kalil, a retired dentist in Methuen, MA and past President of the Massachusetts Dental Society, now spends his time writing poetry among his other hobbies in music and photography. A member of the Grey Court Poets, his poetry has been published in newspapers, magazines, books and journals. "The Dentist's Prayer," which he authored, was accepted by the American Dental Association (ADA) as the universal "Primary Parameter of Care" for dentists to follow in their treatment of patients. It was published in *Chicken Soup for the Dental Soul*, and is found displayed in many dental offices and organizations throughout the country.

This is what he calls an unorthodox book of poetry that he has written. He combines words and thoughts with poetic forms to make for interesting reading. Many of his ideas come from a lifetime of education, teaching, public speaking, writing, TV appearances and as a radio talk show host.

He is devoted to his family and his profession and has vowed to share all of his life experiences with them before his life reaches its expiration date. The book speaks to a philosophy and lifestyle that says life is worth living.

This is the reason for the title "Heaven Can Wait".

Previously Published Poetry

Chicken Soup for the Dental Soul
©1999 by Jack Canfield, Mark Victor Hansen and Don Dibble
"The Dentist's Prayer"

A Trusting Heart
©2000 by the International Library of Poetry as a compilation
"Kelley"

Methuen Life Magazine:

"Thanksgiving Prayer"	November 2013
"Water"	October, 2011
"Winter"	January, 2006

St. Lucy Parish Bulletin:

"Prayer of Thanksgiving"	November 20, 2011
"Parkinson's Prayer"	May 1, 2011

Reviews

"Dr. Kalil with carefully chosen words and rhyme, speaks to universal themes, as he and we with him, travel through life. Thankfulness, family, aging, belief in God and a willingness to gladly meet each day with hope resonate."

Gayle C. Heney: Producer and Host of the TV series Write Now, former Poet Laureate of North Andover, MA

"Dr. Kalil is constantly taking note of the simple things in life and making them seem important, relevant and special through his words. His poetry teaches us to learn from nature, experiences and each other. Even while sometimes writing about difficult subjects, he magnificently combines it with the right amount of humor to make the reader smile. His poetry is easily understandable yet thought-provoking. "Heaven Can Wait" is such a unique piece of art, and it's such a gift to share with family."

Kelley Last: Television Promo Producer for the Hallmark Channel, Los Angeles, CA

38900486R00082

Made in the USA
Middletown, DE
17 March 2019